LEGACIES: Kansas' Older County Courthouses

by
Julie A. Wortman
David P. Johnson
with an introduction by Paul E. Wilson

Kansas State Historical Society, Topeka, Kansas

The Kansas county courthouse survey was financed by the Kansas State Historical Society, the University of Kansas, and the Department of the Interior. However, the contents and opinions do not necessarily reflect the views and opinions of the Department of the Interior.

Photo credits: all photographs contained in this publication were the work of David P. Johnson except for the catalog photograph of the Brown county courthouse, the photograph of the present Clark county courthouse, and the historic photographs, which were obtained from the collections of the Kansas State Historical Society. The catalog photograph of the Meade county courthouse was provided by John Husband, editor of the Meade *Globe-Press.*

Library of Congress Card Catalog Number: 82-81184
ISBN: 0-87726-025-7

Second Printing

Overleaf: Leavenworth county

Cover photos: front, Linn county
back, Sheridan county

Table of Contents

Foreword

County seats and courthouses have long played an important role in Kansas, and American, history. Without the county seat—and/or a railroad—many towns died. With the county seat *and* a railroad many Kansas communities became metropolitan.

Men have fought and died, stolen and cheated to secure the county seat for a particular community. The motive, obviously, was financial.

Most county seats were obtained by rational and honorable means. The names of only the few involved in county seat wars come readily to mind because of their own history.

The point is that county seats were prized possessions which set one town above its peers. Once the rancor produced in locating a county seat, if, indeed, there were any rancor at all, had subsided, city and county residents took pride in the building that represented county government—the courthouse.

Because of pride, the county courthouse was often the most elaborate and striking building in town. Built solidly of stone, concrete, brick, marble, and granite the courthouses were architectural fantasies, castles on the prairie, which signified prosperity, hope, and sense of place.

The material on the following pages illustrates, both graphically and pictorially, the importance of courthouses to Kansas communities. Kansans justifiably take pride in their courthouses and often use them as "homes" when in the county seat on business. This booklet attempts to recognize the place of the county courthouse in the Kansas culture.

I think it succeeds.

JOSEPH W. SNELL
Topeka
September 1, 1981

Riley county

Introduction

by Paul E. Wilson

This publication records an important aspect of the Kansas heritage. All Kansans are indebted to the authors. Here, as elsewhere in America, the county courthouse occupies a unique and honored place in the community that it serves. It has been and continues to be the most visible evidence of our tradition of local self-government under law. Historically the courthouse is the meeting place of government and the governed, the place where those affected by public decisions may be heard and the impact of their views felt, where public scrutiny of the decision making process can be most effective. In an era concerned about the encroachments of bureaucracy, the county courthouse stands as its antithesis.

As I have reached an age when a bit of reminiscence is tolerated, even expected, perhaps I may reflect on my personal relationship with one of the buildings glimpsed in this volume. It began on a cloudy and muggy day in early summer more than 58 years ago when, with my family, I attended ceremonies at which a new courthouse was dedicated. Two years earlier the county commissioners had contracted to pay nearly $200,000 for the construction of a courthouse and an appurtenant jail. It was the county's largest single expenditure until that time. In April, 1923, the new facilities were occupied by the county government.

For weeks before April 27 the prospective dedication of the courthouse had been discussed in the county's newspapers. Billed as the season's biggest celebration, towns, school districts, civic clubs, lodges, patriotic societies, and other organizations were invited to participate. A rain the night before the event was not an unmixed impediment to the festivities, as farmers, who would otherwise be in the fields, were free to take their families to the county seat.

The multi-phased celebration featured a mile-long parade; a barbecue at which one and one half beeves, a barrel of pickles and thousands of buns were consumed; group reunions; boxing matches; courthouse tours; and oratory. The principal speaker was reported to have delivered "a masterly address couched in eloquent language and bringing out many interesting points concerning better government, governmental aims and the purposes to which a courthouse should be dedicated." In the evening there was a free

Clay county

outdoor movie for which we stayed with the result that we got home too late to do the evening milking. But it was a special event—the dedication of a courthouse.

Although the courthouse of the 1920's lacked the richness of detail and the complexity of design found in those built a generation earlier, it was, and probably still is, architecturally the most distinguished building in the county. It sits in the center of a city block, which it shares with the jail and sheriff's residence. Its exterior is of brick and stone. The interior walls and ceilings are of plaster with corridors finished with marble wainscot, terrazzo floors, and ornamental plaster cornices. Stairs and banisters are of marble. Both the facade and the interior reflect the stability and dignity that are appropriate to a place where the important business of county government is conducted.

Twenty-four years later I returned to the courthouse as an officer of the county and for nearly four years I occupied an office there. It was during that period that I was able to observe the unique and critical role of the courthouse in the community.

As its name suggests, the courthouse is first the place where the courts of justice hold their sessions. Traditionally the Anglo-American law has been administered locally to insure that community values are reflected in the dispensing of justice in the community. Here the broad range of judicial business is conducted. Issues involving charges of crime, property rights, family tensions, powers of public officers and the entire spectrum of human controversy are peaceably resolved. This process, the alternative to combat and violence, is the hallmark of a civilized society and the courthouse is its cradle.

The courthouse has other roles in the life of the community. The people go there to pay taxes and protest assessments, to obtain licenses for vehicles, to register to vote, to record instruments affecting important property rights, to petition for improvement of local but vital roads, to seek public financial assistance and on and on. As a boy in my early teens I was a bounty hunter. I hunted gophers and crows, for which the law provided small bounties. At the end of each summer I made a pilgrimage to the courthouse with a basket filled with gopher scalps and crow's bills, collected my bounty payments and enjoyed the pleasant feeling of financial security. Other encounters in the courthouse were more sobering. It was from an office in the courthouse that I received the notice that began four years of wartime military services.

The courthouse was more than the center of county government. Its public rooms were used as meeting places for many community groups. I made my first political speech in the courtroom where I tried my first case. In the absence of a county museum, the corridors of the courthouse provided space for the display of artifacts and documents of local historical interest. Summer brought band concerts and other performances to the courthouse lawn. The courthouse was the site of a considerable amount of social activity. A lot of visiting occurred there, particularly in the sheriff's office. And as not the least of its services, the courthouse provided the only public restrooms in town.

In rural America the courthouse has traditionally been the nucleus and the catalyst of the public life of the community. It was a country courthouse in Mississippi that evoked these lines from the pen of William Faulkner:

> But above all the courthouse; the center, the focus, the hub; sitting, looming in the center of the county's circumference like a single cloud in its ring of horizon, laying its vast shadow to the uttermost rim of the horizon; musing, brooding, symbolic and ponderable, tall as a cloud, solid as a rock, dominating all: protector of the weak, judicate and curb of the passions and lusts, repository and guardian of the aspirations and the hopes.—*Requiem for a Nun*, p. 40.

Although the courthouses of my nostalgia and Faulkner's lyric prose belong to another era, their role has changed only a little in rural communities of Kansas. But urbanization threatens them both physically and functionally. The growth of county business has required new facilities, sometimes resulting in the demolition of the old. Contemporary courthouse builders have, presumably for reasons of economy and efficiency, abandoned the traditions of courthouse architecture. The new buildings, in design and material, are not unlike commercial office buildings. Externally there is little to distinguish them from places where money is borrowed and insurance is sold. The traditional amenities that have made the courthouse a visible monument to local self-government no longer adorn the building from which the county is governed.

Changing concerns in local government and public economy seem to push the traditional county courthouse toward obsolescence. The phrase "energy efficient" and its implications had not been thought of when the courthouses of a few generations ago were designed with lofty ceilings, long, open stairways and broad windows. Courtrooms built at a time when trials were a popular medium of public entertainment are often much too large for today's need, and the traditional design of their working areas is said to be unsuitable for modern litigation. New court service agencies are housed in improvised quarters. Courtrooms are often on the second or third floors of buildings with no elevator service; hence, they are not accessible to the aged and the handicapped.

Non-judicial agencies of government, traditionally located in the courthouse, face demands for expanded service and need for new equipment—but have no place to grow. What are to be the community's responses to the inadequacy of the courthouse? Demolition and replacement? Augmentation? Conversion to another use?

For some of us,. the nostalgic appeal of old courthouses goes a long way toward justifying preservation. But the practical economics of county government require that there be better reasons. As construction costs rise and the need for conserving society's resources becomes increasingly apparent, the continued use of sturdy, durable old buildings seems highly practicable. Remodeling to utilize unused space or augmentation with new facilities may be possible answers. If use for judicial or governmental purposes is no longer feasible, adaption to other appropriate uses might serve a public need. It should never be forgotten that the courthouse is, more than any other, a place where local history has been made. The community owes it to its traditions, its history, its self, and to future generations that it not demolish its courthouse peremptorily.

For those whose favorite courthouse does not survive, this book may provide a pleasant reminder of times that were.

Paul E. Wilson is Kane Professor of Law, University of Kansas.

Court

An Atmosphere of Dignity and Calm

A Photographic Essay by David P. Johnson

Leavenworth county

Franklin county

"The county's business for forty years has been scattered over the city, now every county officer is housed under one roof."

Chase county

Chase county

Atchison county

Clay county

Chase county

"The iron cornice for the courthouse has arrived and will be put in place as soon as possible. It will crown the structure beautifully."

Wichita county

Wyandotte county

Sedgwick county (old)

"There were two principal factors to begin with: The erection of a building that would in every way be a credit to the community and the expenditure of the least possible amount of money to secure that result."

Sedgwick county (old)

Miami county

Harper county

Chautauqua county

Chase county

"It was copied from an old English court room according to one learned young man, and is very impressive."

Linn county

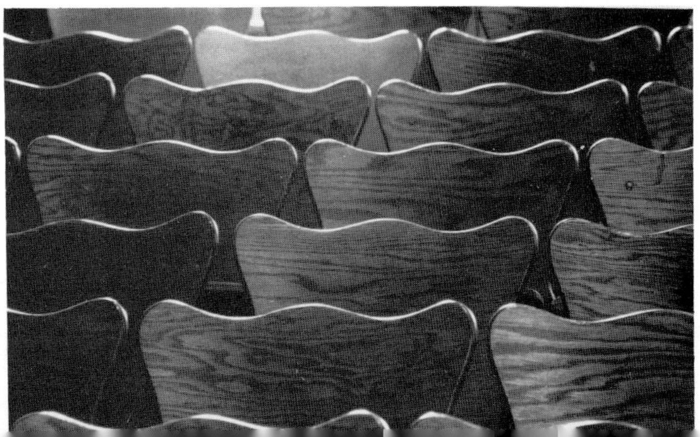

Miami county

Logan county (old)

Ness county

Reno county

Kiowa county

"After looking the building over you will say that you do not see how it could have been built for the money."

Mitchell county

Rush county

Stafford county

Washington county

Lincoln county

Ness county

David P. Johnson was an assistant professor of journalism at the University of Kansas, at the time he worked on the Kansas county courthouse survey and this publication. He is currently employed by the National Geographic Society.

Douglas county

"The Topeka court house, built of Colorado stone, will cost $138,000 unfurnished, and is too fancy for the Atchison County men, who have a tendency to the home spun."

Linn county

Wabaunsee county

Harper county

Legacies: Kansas' Older County Courthouses

by Julie A. Wortman

County governments play an important role in Kansas. They effectively respond to needs which neither state nor local governments are designed to meet. Because the county is an important unit in the hierarchy of governmental organizations, the county courthouse is respected as a seat of legal authority and public service.

Traditionally, the building constructed to serve as the permanent facility for the storage of county records, for the conduct of county business, and for the administration of justice has been considered a tangible symbol of the county—brick, stone, tower and portico joined together to form an idealized architectural self-portrait. One of the orators participating in the dedication of the Franklin county courthouse in 1893 expressed this idea clearly. "Into these ample halls," he predicted, "all shall invite our friends, and let the beauty and solidity of the structure speak of the social harmony and material prosperity of Franklin county." [1] The enthusiastic comment of a Brown county citizen is also typical: "The well-being and good taste of its people and the wealth of its good earth are reflected in Brown County's courthouse." [2] Courthouses constructed of locally quarried limestone communicate a vivid likeness of the county in geological terms, but a more graphic expression of the idea that the courthouse portrays the county has appeared in recent decades: stone maps carved to display county boundaries and communities have been incorporated into the main wall of the new courthouses or sometimes set up as a free-standing sign.

County citizens have always endeavored to secure a building that projects both a prosperous image and a thoroughly modern outlook. A reporter for the Kinsley *Mercury* found the desired combination in the new Edwards county courthouse in 1929. His account declared it to be a "fine monument of the prosperity of the county," and "up-to-date in all details." [3] The objective evidently was also met in Butler county. After praising the new building in El Dorado, an observer said, "Butler is the largest, wealthiest, and grandest county in the state. The people are out of debt, live in modern homes, are God fearing, country loving, bright faced, well dressed, happy and prosperous; they ride in autos, buggies, in 'one horse

Wyandotte county

shays,' horseback and any other way they please and when flying machines are perfected they will use them." [4] If not every admirer of his county's new courthouse believed he might one day take to the skies, it seems always to have been taken for granted that a new courthouse evidenced a county's flourishing compatibility with the modern world.

The 34 county courthouses in Kansas that have been constructed since 1941 are the most recent expressions of the cherished ideal of modernity in county courthouses. In 1958 the *Kansas Government Journal* assessed the new courthouses, finding that each was "much like any other modern office building." [5] This tendency to design courthouses that look like office buildings has continued to the present. Without paying careful attention to signs or other secondary clues, one often finds it difficult to distinguish the most recently constructed facilities from the medical or insurance building down the street. The office building is only a slightly less characteristic architectural image of our day than is the drive-in bank, so it is small wonder that county governments should choose today to house themselves in what might be termed temples of efficiency.

The 75 courthouses constructed before 1941 that still remain in Kansas were intended to facilitate the efficient conduct of county business just as their modern counterparts, but their appearance sets them apart from more modern architecture. They no longer look "up-to-date." This raises an interesting question. If possessing a courthouse that projects a modern image has been so important, why haven't most of these older buildings been replaced by now?

Doubtless, a number are already scheduled to be superseded by new facilities. But, many are likely to survive for some time because of factors that stem from their historic character. In fact, the older county courthouses in Kansas offer four legacies which argue for their preservation. These are a material legacy, and legacies of culture, beauty, and inspiration. Appreciation of some or all of these has led to the survival of these buildings until today. The extent to which these legacies continue to be appreciated will determine the future of these structures, perhaps even at the cost of abandoning the traditional courthouse ideal.

Material Legacy

"The old building was a very fine one for this part of the state when it was built," acknowledged a Hodgeman county reporter in 1929, "but the needs of the county have long since outgrown it, and the ever increasing danger of fire was taken into consideration in making plans for the new one." [6] He could have been writing about virtually any Kansas courthouse that has been replaced. The new county courthouse invariably has been constructed to correct the perceived deficiencies of the previous one. Whether in protest against overcrowded quarters in the upper stories of commercial buildings or in modest frame structures hastily constructed and donated by a town company to win county seat designation, or whether in response to the damage left by storms or fires, the new courthouse has always been an endeavor in safe, solid, commodious construction.

Clark county courthouse old (1888) and new (1951)—each generation has its own idea of how a courthouse should look.

The old Thomas county courthouse was considered a fire trap, prompting construction of the present courthouse in 1906.

The hope and conviction that the new foundations would prove firm and lasting were symbolized by Masonic ceremonies at the laying of the cornerstone. The Anthony *Bulletin* expected that "on this foundation there should rise a building which would be an ornament to the city and a beautiful and useful temple for the use of the people of the whole county." [7] Such was the concern in Harper county that the new courthouse be a "safe and sensible building" that foundation footings were made deeper and thicker at the insistence of concerned citizens, although the architect assured them that his specifications had been adequate.

Reports on the quality of courthouse construction were eagerly filed as new buildings went up. In Linn county welcome confirmation of the soundness of the new courthouse came when this report appeared in the *Linn County Clarion* in 1886: "The walls are said, by masons and architects who have seen them, to be the best ever erected in the west." [8]

Aside from making certain that the new courthouse was structurally stable, county officials wanted to be assured that the overcrowding and inconvenience which had plagued them would not soon trouble them again. In anticipation of further growth most courthouses were planned with ample extra space. The 1917 Chautauqua county courthouse, like many others, was "built to accommodate the county with twice the population that now exists." [9] Likewise, in 1926, the new Stanton county courthouse was said to be "large and roomy," so as to "adequately house the county officers and take care of county needs for years to come." [10]

Making county records safe from fire was another typical preoccupation for those planning new courthouses. The bitter experience of devastating fires in many counties made alarmists of almost everyone, and the need for better fireproofing proved a convincing argument for constructing many new facilities. "The old courthouse is a fire trap where every record belonging to the county might be destroyed any time," complained the Colby *Free Press* in 1905. "This would not only necessitate a new house but it would jeopardize the title of almost every piece of land in the county. The farmers in the county realize this and so far have been heard from to a man for the new building." [11]

A fireproof courthouse was a source of great pride. In Ford county, when the 1913 courthouse was completed, self-congratulations were passed around as

Stone foundations laid in 1885 still support the Linn county courthouse.

The Lincoln county courthouse is constructed of post rock, a type of limestone native to the county.

the Dodge City *Daily Globe* headlined the news that "Only One Other Court House in Kansas Is Absolutely Fireproof—The Dodge Building Will Be the Model in Western Kansas." [12] Reportedly, the only wood in the building was that of the handrails and office doors. Indeed, the history of county courthouse construction has been in part a tale of the progressive elimination of wood as a structural or finish material. Wood beams, rafters, joists, and studs were eventually replaced by iron, steel, or reinforced concrete members. Ceramic tiles and then, more commonly, reinforced concrete slabs were used in ceilings and floors. Before flat roofs became popular, slate, rather than wood shingles or metal sheathings, had become the preferred roofing material. Wall and floor surfaces that had once been adorned with wood wainscoting and flooring were faced with tile, stone, or terrazzo (a material made of cement and marble ground to a smooth finish).

Many of the courthouses which previous generations of county officials labored to make sound, commodious, and fireproof remain sufficiently so that with only relatively minor adjustments they continue to be suited to their purpose. This material legacy has been valued in practical terms. Max Anderson, "a Beloit boy, born and bred," could have been speaking for the youth in many other counties when he pointed to his own county's new courthouse in 1901 and vowed, "the younger generation wish to assure you that they appreciate your labors. They will neither waste nor will they destroy." [13] Even in the absence of such vows, the older courthouses will continue to be used as long as they are structurally sound, possess sufficient space, and are safe. Economy is vital to the operation of county government and was one of the ruling factors in construction of the older buildings. "There is no question that the county received the worth of the money expended and have a

The builders of the 1890 Greeley county courthouse hoped it would last for several generations.

building that will serve as the home of the officers elected by the people for several generations to come at a minimum of costs," observed the *Greeley County Journal* in 1890.[14] Likewise, this watchful concern that public funds be expended prudently led to an enthusiastic report which appeared in the *Smith County Pioneer* in 1920: "After looking the building over you will say that you do not see how it could have been built and furnished for the money. The commissioners certainly have allowed no graft and have figured the furnishings and materials down to the lowest notch." [15]

The chance to continue to capitalize on the investment of 60 or more years ago is seldom given up, but adopting the tradition of the "lowest notch" of expenditure in maintaining the courthouse building has meant the certain erosion of the initial investment. Superficial repairs or cosmetic cover-up schemes have left many of the older buildings looking more decrepit than they might actually be. And, the reluctance to spend funds on adequate maintenance and repair has led in some cases to urgent needs for either expensive rehabilitation work or, more expensive still, replacement.

Cultural Legacy

Those who constructed the older county courthouses hoped that the buildings would endure for a good many years and many of the contemporary accounts suggest they also hoped that they were building a valuable heritage for posterity. Of what was such a legacy to consist? Their thoughts on this score seem vague, though the heritage they hoped to pass on through the courthouse may have involved a conviction that the building reflected their personal achievements.

While those predecessors may not have realized it, their emphasis on securing a courthouse that was "up-to-date" in every respect resulted in buildings that reflect certain aspects of Kansas' cultural history. The buildings they constructed bore witness to the values of the times in which they lived. "Style" is the term commonly used to denote the characteristics which unite buildings designed according to a particular frame of mind. Kansas' county courthouses have been designed using the formal language of a variety of different architectural styles. These architectural styles remind one of the different frames of mind that produced them and rendered them popular. The absence of certain architectural styles, too, reminds one that Kansas was settled later than 33 other states.

It is not clear how much the patrons of a new courthouse really understood architectural style. For example, the "Queen Anne" design of the Linn county courthouse may or may not have been recognized to have something to do with a rejection of High Victorian morality and the aesthetics of harsh formal contrasts, on one hand, and an affirmation of a more relaxed moral view and the aesthetics of "quaintness," on the other. How many citizens of Kansas knew of Boston architect Henry Hobson Richardson, whose work was the basis for the Romanesque revival courthouses erected in such abundance here? And as Kansans erected modern classical eclectic designs loosely patterned after Renaissance palaces did they imagine themselves to be part of the great new architectural tradition that the critic and historian Talbot Hamlin and others envisioned?

It is unlikely that many citizens knew much about architectural style except to understand what was most fashionable. The few discussions about style to be found in older newspaper accounts of courthouse projects either brush over that aspect with a quick comment on what the architect termed the design or present a confusing explanation. When the massive rebuilding of the Leavenworth county courthouse was being planned in 1911, the talk revolved around how the new courthouse would be designed "along simple, graceful lines entirely absent of any of the 'gingerbread' effects." [16] When the architect, William Feth, presented a building "of classical design, with straight lines predominating," citizens asked for "something after the Spanish mission style." [17] Feth obliged, but the result is hardly anything like what

The 1873 Leavenworth county courthouse was gutted by fire in 1911. The new courthouse was built using the same foundation and some of the walls.

one could call mission style, except that arches were used instead of straight lines.

County commissioners would often select an architectural style for the new courthouse that was no longer especially popular among the leading architects. Perhaps this is indicative of a certain conservatism in those counties, but just as likely it demonstrates that the *avant-garde* is seldom assimilated as quickly as appreciative critics wish. Also, many of the courthouse designs appear to be stylistic hybrids. Whether this can be attributed to the designer's failure to understand completely the architectural style he had chosen or as a sign of independence and creativity, is seldom clear. Sometimes it seems that while the designer (or client?) was drawn to certain aspects of a new style, he was reluctant to abandon the beloved features of an older one. Many of the courthouses designed by Ottawa architect George P. Washburn, for example, display classical/colonial revival features—palladian windows, delicate cupolas, porticoes—within the context of Romanesque revival styling. The result is refreshing and distinctive.

If the architectural styles of the older courthouses link them to distinctive periods in history, the cultural legacy they offer also stems from associations with persons and events over a long period of time. These form an evocative patina which transforms the older buildings into entities which are the creations of their builders and also their keepers.

Historically the county courthouse was often referred to as the "county house," and like the hereditary home of a large family, its grounds, hallways, courtroom, and offices acquired the mementos and trophies of successive generations of county citizens. Not only records, but memories are stored here. A portrait of General Pershing still hangs in the corridor of the courthouse in Cottonwood Falls and a 1918 Salvation Army poster advertising the United War Work Campaign remains on display at the Rooks county courthouse. These are not the only reminders

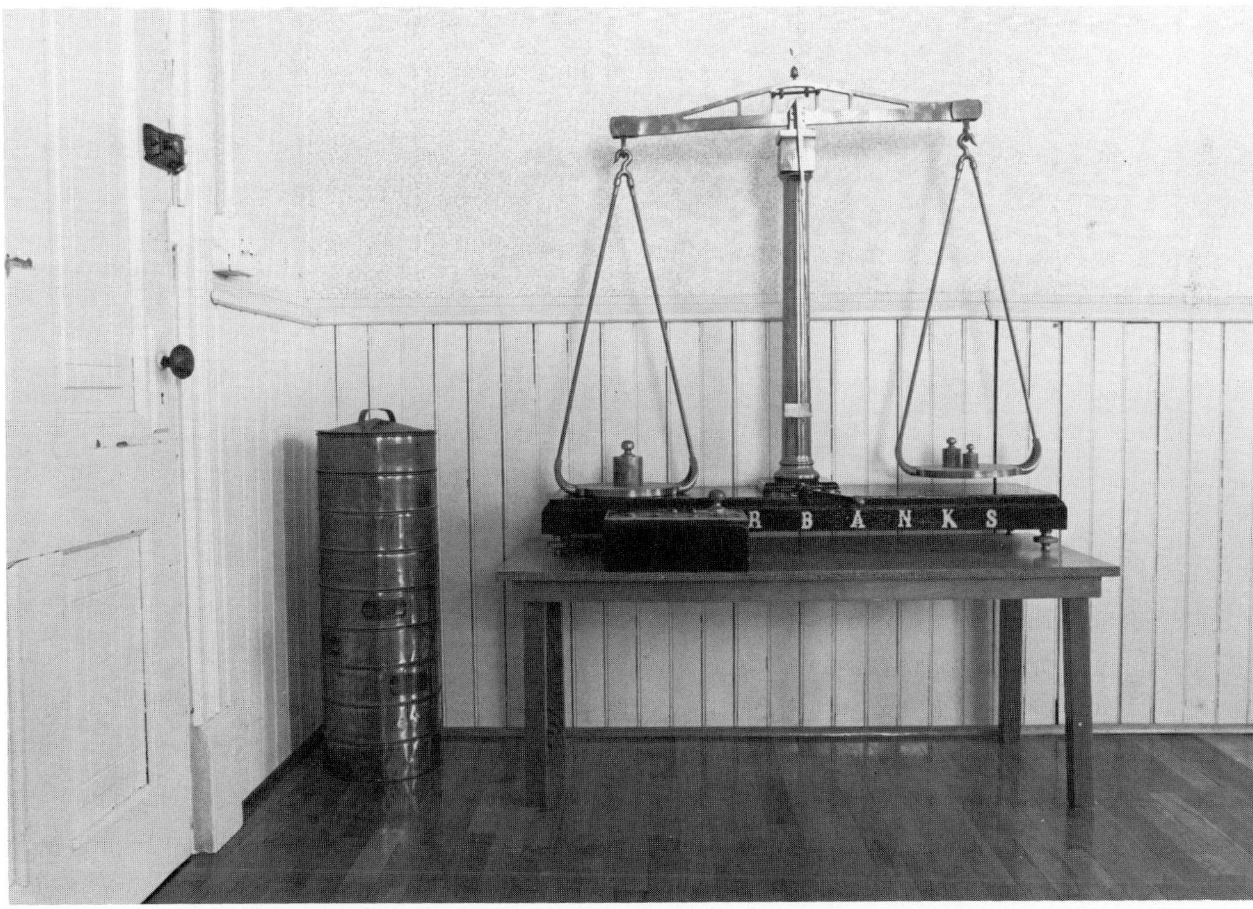

A set of scales and measures formerly employed to check the accuracy of weights and measures used in the county is still on hand at the Comanche county courthouse.

of events which claimed the devotion and lives of county citizens. Memorials dedicated to the county men who served with the Grand Army of the Republic, with Teddy Roosevelt, Eisenhower, and Patton adorn lobbies and courthouse lawns, erected by generations of county school children and civic organizations. Images of the judges who have presided in the courtroom over the decades look down from the walls. The horns of elk and the stuffed heads of bison, some of these animals notorious in county history, share exhibit space with cherished rock collections and the artifacts of early life on the prairie.

The old "county house" idea had a literal meaning, too. When they come to conduct some piece of business today, county citizens probably spend less time in the courthouse than did their ancestors. But when a journey to the county seat could consume an entire day, citizens would make the courthouse their headquarters—their "home away from home." The large restrooms to be found in many courthouse basements were planned to accommodate women and children weary from traveling or shopping. "The farmers' assembly room is conveniently located and adjoining this is the ladies rest room both of which rooms are intended for the use of the public so that warm apartments will always be open to those who may have long drives from the outside districts, especially with children," reported the Howard *Courant* in 1907 of the proposed courthouse for Elk county.[18] It was suggested in Harper county that the ladies' rest room in the new courthouse in Anthony be supplied with a record player and John Philip Sousa records for the pleasure of the weary. A Larned newspaper boasted that "One of the most handsome rooms in the new courthouse, and one which probably will be used a great deal is the ladies rest room on the first floor." In 1919 Pawnee county could afford the best for its women: "It is furnished with mirror, writing desk, tables, settees, etc., and handsome decorations in the way of curtains, rugs, etc. The room will seat at least

Old posters are mementos of the past which hang on the walls of some courthouses. This one can be found at the Wabaunsee county courthouse.

An unusual relationship of fixtures in the men's restroom at the Elk county courthouse is the result of efforts to integrate modern needs with the 1907 building.

This early view of the 1887 Logan county courthouse suggests what a major accomplishment erecting a courthouse could be in a sparsely settled county.

fifty persons. The furniture is reed, with tapestry upholstery. This room will be open to the public, of course, and is expected to fill a long felt want among the women who can make this their headquarters when they come to town, while their husbands are attending to their affairs." [19]

Today few women or men spend hours on end at the courthouse, resting and visiting with their neighbors from around the county. But in the counties which have remained sparsely populated, the county house image in this sense of the courthouse as a second home still survives. On a wintry day in Sharon Springs one finds the courthouse serving as a comfortable winter home for plants brought in by citizens of Wallace county who haven't room for them inside. And many courthouse corridors are still the congenial setting for frequent reunions of friends. Maintaining close ties with one's neighbors is still important in many counties, perhaps out of a feeling for what made the county an important institution. This idea was expressed well by the women of Logan county, who wished all county citizens to attend the 1887 dedication of the courthouse in Russell Springs: "Pioneers in a land remote from old-time friendships and associations, our people desire closer acquaintance with those who must vie with them in efforts to establish social and educational systems in the grand new county of their adoption." [20]

When the older building finally has been deemed too small or too decrepit for the efficient conduct of county business, sentiment for the heritage offered by the county house, for the familiar and pleasant feeling of rubbing shoulders with a personal and public past, has been known to counsel preservation rather than demolition. Sometimes, the old building becomes an annex to a new one, or vice versa, and sometimes the building is set aside as a museum or used for other purposes. More frequently, heritage is likely to secure only a partial victory. Bits and pieces of the old building—the old tower clock, the plaques, and portraits—are salvaged and displayed with the new facility, or something like what happened in Alma in 1932 takes place: "The city razed the old building, saving as much of the usable materials as

The clock was salvaged and transformed into a monument when the old Allen county courthouse was demolished in 1957.

possible and selling it. Much of the front face stone will go into buildings, becoming mementos and lasting souvenirs of the old courthouse." [21]

The ideal of having a courthouse that represents the prosperous modernity of the county has traditionally overruled the feeling that the old building has become meaningful in other terms. "In the removal of the old court house," wrote a Grant county observer in 1930, "one of the familiar land marks will go. It has done its duty and, no doubt, if the old building could speak, it would do as many of us are doing today, congratulating the present county commissioners on the splendid edifice that marks the site of the old court house." [22]

Legacy of Beauty

When it is proposed today to replace an old courthouse, those aligning themselves against the costly proposition often include persons who argue that the old building offers a legacy of uniqueness and beauty that makes it too valuable to destroy. While a new building might be aesthetically satisfying in modern terms, the old buildings offer design characteristics which are deemed refreshing alternatives to the new architecture.

Although sometimes buildings have been built that are unique within the context of the architecture of their age, public buildings have usually been designed according to the dictates of one of the nationally or regionally accepted styles of the day. Maverick designs are unlikely to win the approval of a majority of voters, and county commissioners, at least, have been concerned that such approval be given.

What appears unique about many of the old courthouses has more to do with the fact that some of them are lone survivors of their age or stylistic family. The courthouses in Westmoreland, Cottonwood Falls, Tribune (the old Greeley county courthouse), Mound City, and Russell Springs (the old Logan county courthouse) are reminders of what many other courthouses in Kansas looked like, although only these buildings remain to exhibit the distinctive stylistic characteristics of the earlier times.

Uniqueness can also be attributed to some older courthouses even though there are others still surviving that share the same basic style of design because certain features set them apart from their peers. The differences between similar designs, though, are likely to be minor. When asked to compare his design for the Clay county courthouse with

The new Marshall county courthouse has left the old courthouse available for other uses.

The 1873 courthouse that once served Greenwood county was designed by John Haskell according to plans very similar to those used at the Chase county courthouse.

his designs for the courthouses at Burlington and Beloit, the architect J. C. Holland remarked, "the size of all three buildings, style and treatment are about the same, except more carving and cut stone on yours than either of the others, the central tower necessitating extra expense." [23]

Too much uniqueness would not have been especially desirable. This was not solely out of deference to the tastes of a majority of county citizens. Counties vied for something better, if possible, but at least for something comparable to the new courthouses their neighbors possessed. County commissioners, entrusted with the responsibility for selecting the design for the county's new courthouse, commonly followed the practice of visiting counties with newly constructed buildings to collect ideas for their own future courthouse. Often they returned home enamored of a particular building or of the work of a particular architect. In the case of commissioners planning new courthouses in the 1890's and early 1900's, more often than not the commission would go to either J. C. Holland or G. P. Washburn. Perhaps the work of these two men, both working in the idiom of the Romanesque revival, was unusually well attuned to the tastes of their day, or possibly they simply had the right connections. It is also likely that they were skilled at capitalizing on inter-county rivalries. The result was that nearly every courthouse constructed during this period was a variation of either Holland's or Washburn's basic Romanesque revival prototype. The clients were pleased with the result. The following account, filed in 1907, presents a typical case, here involving Holland's selection as architect for the new Osborne county courthouse: "J. C. Holland, an architect of Topeka was here and met the Board. Mr. Holland is one of the best architects in the west. He furnished the plans and specifications for the courthouses at Clay Center, Junction City, Manhattan and Newton and at all of these places the county commissioners and officers speak in the highest terms of his work. Mr. Holland has been asked by the board to submit specifications for the new building and it is probable that his plans will be accepted . . . the new building will as near as practicable be like the court houses at Manhattan and Newton, which will give Osborne a court house of which every citizen may be justly proud." [24]

Many people mourn the changes which have taken place in aesthetic tastes since the old buildings were constructed. Even if the old courthouses were not especially unique when they were constructed, nor especially unique when compared to similar surviving work, they are deemed aesthetically valuable. Visiting some of these older buildings can indeed be a treat. Inside, oak and other hardwoods can be found trimming doors, serving as wainscoting and floor boards, or worked into benches, counters, and chairs. Polished marble or colorful glazed tilework covers the floor surfaces and walls of many corridors. Pressed metal ceilings also survive in some buildings, supplying an ornamental texture for these surfaces which is a pleasant change from the now-common suspended systems. Lowered ceilings in courtrooms have hidden many stained-glass lunettes from view, but in some instances colored glass arranged in compositions depicting symbols of the law can still be enjoyed. Stained-glass skylights and domes cast a splendid light in a few corridors and lobbies. In some instances murals present Justice enthroned in august splendor. Ornamental cornices and pilasters provide eye-catching detail. Grand staircases often conduct one to grand spaces—whether to Wyandotte county's barrel vaulted corridor, to a two-story courtroom by Washburn, or to the rotunda of the Leavenworth county courthouse. In Reno county, one is overwhelmed by the vast expanse of the main office area which rises two stories in the center of the building.

Outside, the landscaped courthouse square often lends a pleasant park-like feeling to the site. On the exterior of the buildings stonework and brickwork of

County commissioners were the people responsible for looking after the details of constructing a new courthouse. Seen here are the Graham county commissioners and county clerk in 1922.

Architects James C. Holland (*left*) and George P. Washburn (*right*) each received numerous courthouse commissions in Kansas during the turn-of-the-century period.

high quality craftsmanship can also be found. At the old Douglas county courthouse the variety of stonework utilized is as impressive as it is eye-catching. Elsewhere, amusing sculptural ornament enlivens entrances and other focal points of the architectural design. Ornamental cornices and cartouches catch the sun, forming expressive shadows.

Of course, many of the older courthouses are quite plain, especially inside. But this very spartan appearance can also be aesthetically appealing.

Architectural beauty is, of course, a desirable attribute for a county courthouse, or for any building. But aesthetic arguments for sensitive preservation measures are unlikely to weigh heavily with county officials preoccupied with keeping county operations safely housed in the most up-to-date fashion possible. Attending to aesthetics seems to many officials too costly, too troublesome, too inessential. Solutions to energy inefficiency, to acoustical difficulties, and to the need for space are usually lifted from techniques developed for new construction and as a result these solutions have compromised the original design characteristics of many of the older buildings.

Legacy of Inspiration

Finally, some of those who have defended the old courthouses have done so because they feel that the old buldings offer a legacy of inspiration. In part this has to do with the structural solidity which is evidenced by many of these buildings and which has caused the practical-minded to retain them. In part, too, it has to do with the sense of heritage they inspire. But it also has partly to do with a feeling that many of them are aesthetically pleasing. This point of view also involves an inclination to affirm the basic value which shaped the older courthouses—the conviction that county government should not only serve, but should enjoy special recognition as an agency charged with the responsibility of maintaining the high values of a democratic society.

Reno county business is conducted in this impressive two-story space in the 1930 courthouse.

In some respects, the style chosen for the older buildings was meant, and taken, to express this notion. But most styles have at their heart lofty ideals anyway, judging from what the critics have written about them. So style alone cannot necessarily account for the special sense that the older courthouses seem to be especially like what county courthouses should be. The appraisal of the Bourbon county courthouse contained in a report on the county's facilities prepared in 1938 hints at the quality many feel transcends style: "The exterior of the building itself is built upon extreme simplicity. Of classic design, the dominant note outside is the Corinthian columns that sweep upward from the first story at the front of the building. There are but few curves on the exterior design, most of them being at the ends of the columns, and the subsequent severity of the building gives it an atmosphere of dignity and calm." [25]

"Dignity and calm" seems a good way to express the feeling supplied by many older courthouse designs. Implied is a sense of aloofness from the trivialities and mundane concerns which sets the courthouse apart as a place where activities of grave substance transpire.

The designers of the older buildings capitalized, in most cases, on the fact that Kansas courthouses were usually accorded a generous block of land for the site. Thus secluded from immediate encroachment, they literally stand apart from the other buildings in town. The townsite company or private citizens of the county seat community may have donated the land for the courthouse, to secure the county seat designation or to insure that flow of traffic to the courthouse would be circulated through the commercial district. However, the courthouse sitting on its spacious site in the middle of the downtown, or at the end of the main street or a block or two behind it, seems profoundly distinct from the hustle and bustle of the commercial world. This feeling is enhanced where the site has been landscaped with attention to an effect of monumentality, or of a park-like atmosphere. In some cases the courthouse can even be

The old jail at the Stafford county courthouse has been imaginatively transformed into a law library.

seen from a considerable distance, calling attention to what, after all, is the special distinction of the county seat.

The older buildings themselves, however small, manage to seem imposing. Tower, portico, or colonnade are devices used to give breadth and focus to the main facade. Almost always one must climb a stairs to gain access to the main floor because the building is usually set above a basement story that is either fully or partially above grade. Once inside, wide corridors, broad staircases, and majestic courtrooms emphasize the main purpose of the county government—the path to the courtroom, and therefore to justice, receives the primary emphasis. Offices are set aside, off the main corridors.

Certain of Kansas' older courthouses seem to have been preserved because the old buildings continue to express for county citizens the values which they were built to affirm. The courthouse at Anthony is an outstanding example. It has been carefully maintained and repaired over the years to conserve every aspect of the dignity and beauty of the original design. Modern needs have been accommodated without conflicting with the character of the historic building. Here one feels keenly that growth has been as much a matter of conservation as of expansion and modernization.

In conclusion, as long as the older county courthouses are appreciated for the legacies they offer, whether of material, culture, aesthetics, or inspiration, they have a chance of surviving beyond the present into the future. But the traditional ideal of a county courthouse that is strictly modern will undoubtedly continue to present a formidable obstacle to their preservation.

Kansas' historic preservation law gives Kansans the opportunity to encourage the physical preservation of the older courthouses if that is feasible. For those reluctant to lose the material, historic, aesthetic, and inspirational legacies offered by the older courthouses, this is good news. But if the law encourages preservation, it cannot guarantee it. Accordingly, the key question is whether a county will take an affirmative position when it comes to conserving its older courthouse. An affirmation of the importance of the older courthouses will mean a transformation of the old ideal of modernity, with preservation serving not as an alternative to modernity, but as a part of it.

Julie A. Wortman is an architectural historian employed as a Historic Preservation Specialist II, by the Historic Preservation Department, Kansas State Historical Society.

Footnotes

1. Ottawa *Weekly Republican,* October 5, 1893.
2. Woman's Kansas Day Club, "Courthouse of 1879, Brown County," 1948 (Ms., Kansas State Historical Society Library).
3. Kinsley *Mercury,* May 30, 1929.
4. *History of Butler County and the New Court House* (Hitchcock Triple Stores, El Dorado, n.d.).
5. "Modernistic Trend Replaces Ornate in New Courthouse Buildings," *Kansas Government Journal,* August, 1958, p. 446.
6. Jetmore *Republican,* January 11, 1929.
7. Anthony *Bulletin,* January 31, 1908.
8. *Linn County Clarion,* Mound City, October 8, 1886.
9. Sedan *Times-Star,* July 12, 1917.
10. Johnson City *Pioneer and Journal News,* September 10, 1926.
11. Colby *Free Press,* September 28, 1905.
12. Dodge City *Daily Globe,* March 17, 1913.
13. Beloit *Gazette,* November 28, 1901.
14. *Greeley County Journal,* Tribune, December 18, 1890.
15. *Smith County Pioneer,* Smith Center, January 1, 1920.
16. Leavenworth *Weekly Times,* August 17, 1911.
17. *Ibid.,* August 24, 1911.
18. Howard *Courant,* April 12, 1907.
19. Larned *Tiller and Toiler,* April 24, 1919.
20. *Logan County Leader,* Russell Springs, December 8, 1887.
21. Alma *Signal,* April 28, 1932.
22. *Grant County Republican,* Ulysses, September 25, 1930.
23. Clay Center *Dispatch,* October 31, 1901.
24. *Osborne County News,* Osborne, February 14, 1907.
25. Works Progress Administration Historical Records Survey, "Bourbon County: Housing, Care and Accessibility of Records," June 3, 1938 (Archives, Kansas State Historical Society).

Laying the cornerstone for the 1896 courthouse was a festive occasion in Topeka.

COUNTY CLERK

The County House

A Photographic Essay by David P. Johnson

JUDGE CHARLES E. WORDEN — Norton county

JUDITH A. CRISMAS, COUNTY CLERK
Anderson county

Rawlins county

JUDGE WILLIAM L. STEVENSON Doniphan county

JUDGE CHARLES M. WARREN Miami county

JUDGE MAURICE L. JOHNSON Gray county

MAGISTRATE JUDGE JOHN MOORE Harper county

JUDGE J. W. LAWRY

Atchison county

"The probate judge thinks that the new courthouse will help his business, at any rate the matrimonial part, which is lagging right now."

Osborne county

"All of the county offices may now be found in cozy quarters in the new court house."

Phillips county

Mitchell county

Osborne county

Lincoln county

"Will Tran has blood poison in his hand resulting from a bruise while working on the stone work at the court house."

VERNON E. VINCENT, SHERIFF — Wallace county

IONE BROWN, COUNTY TREASURER, AND SNOOPY
Wallace county

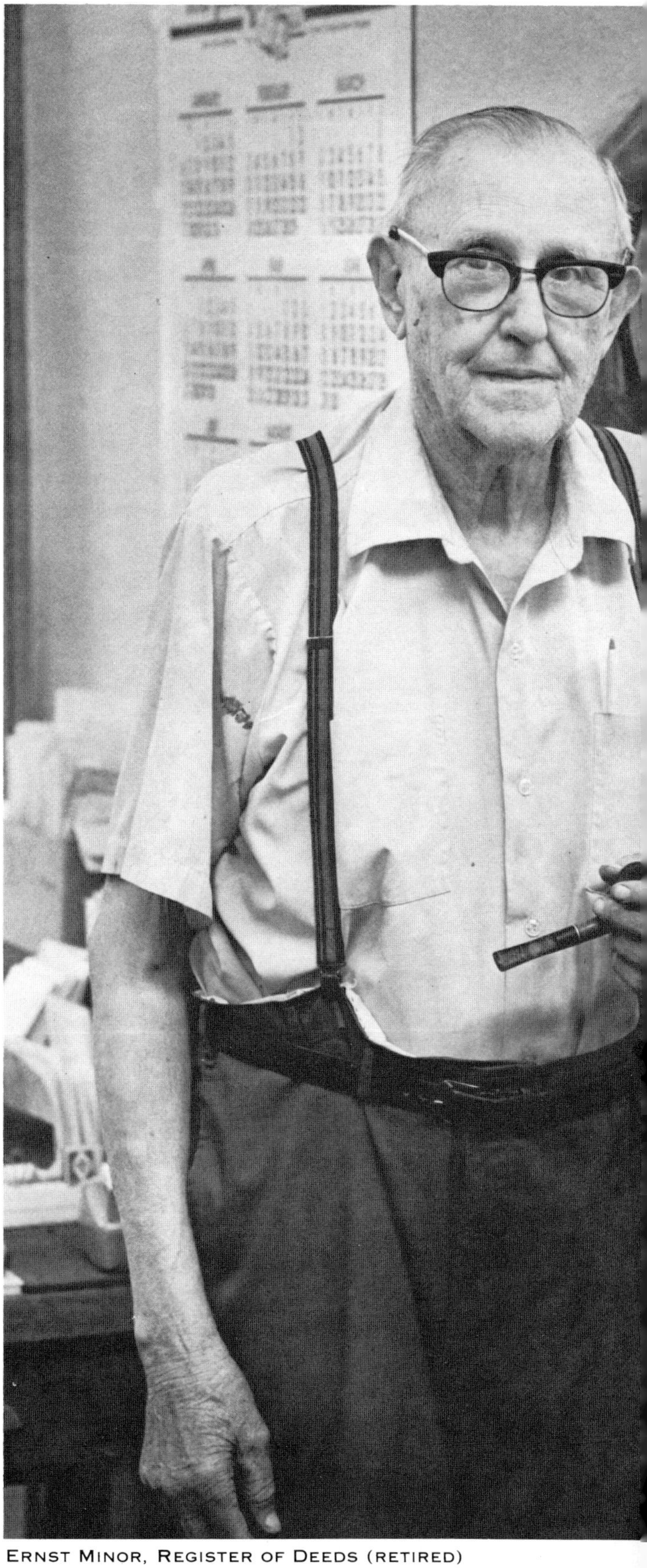

ERNST MINOR, REGISTER OF DEEDS (RETIRED)

Wichita county

VERGIE WENTE, CLERK OF DISTRICT COURT

Sheridan county

GAYLE BAINTER, COUNTY ASSESSOR

Sheridan county

"There is only one thing that can make any man regret voting for a new court house last Tuesday and that is a series of hard years, and failure of crops. . . ."

Logan county (old)

Rooks county

Rooks county

Smith county

Lane county

"The court house will last a long time and the tax payers want something good."

Jackson county

Chase county

Thomas county

HARVEY R. HOLMES AND PHILIP MILLER

Miami county

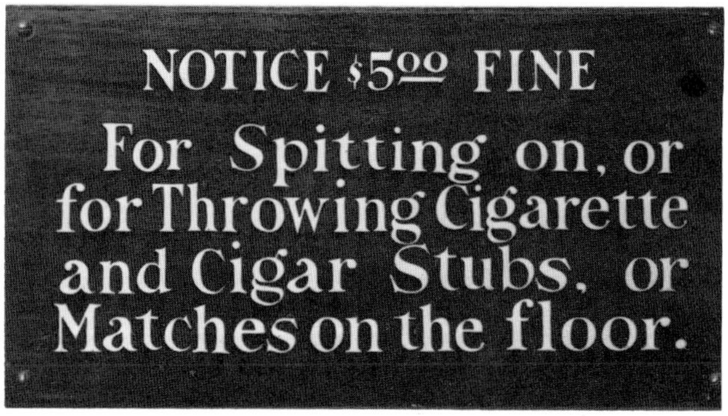

Washington county

NORBERT MAREK — Pottawatomie county

MR. AND MRS. JOHN KING — Republic county

CHARLES L. "PAPPY" PEIRCE — Riley county

HERBERT WARREN
Osage county

Finney county

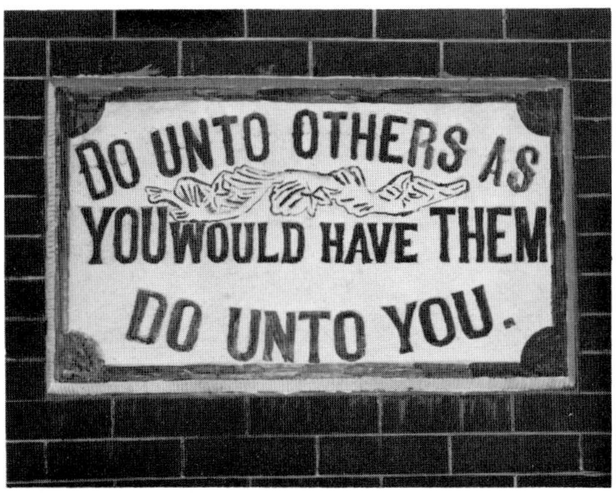

Woodson county

EUGENE HESTON

Atchison county

Mitchell county

Osborne county

Washington county

Wyandotte county

Sedgwick county (old)

"The move toward having a court house square or beautiful city park is still being pushed."

Montgomery county

Rawlins county

Riley county

Catalog: Kansas' Older County Courthouses

Courthouse buildings included in the catalog are structures originally constructed to be permanent county courthouse facilities before 1941 which continue on the exterior, at least, to evidence clearly their historic character. Where a building's original design has been substantially altered, but the later appearance is also historically meaningful, the building has been included, with the catalog entry pertaining to the design as altered.

The dates given refer to the beginning and ending dates of construction. Parenthetical references are made if a courthouse design was drawn up considerably earlier than the period of construction. No attempt has been made to resolve the inconsistencies in the names of architects or contractors which are apparent when different entries are compared. The names given are in the form obtained from the historical sources consulted. Stylistic designations appear in quotation marks if the term was used historically. Terms undistinguished by quotation marks are modern designations.

When a courthouse building no longer serves as the courthouse nor contains county offices, it is parenthetically referred to as "old courthouse." The term "contractor" is used to refer to the firm or individual who was chiefly involved in constructing the building, even if, strictly speaking, not as a contractor. In referring to trim material, the chief ornamenting trim material is identified.

Anderson

Atchison

ANDERSON COUNTY, Garnett
1901-1902
George P. Washburn, architect
Latimer & Benning, contractor
Romanesque Revival. Occupies full block square surrounded on three sides by the central business district; red brick with limestone trim; statue of "Justice" above main entrance; courtroom has been shortened with minimal loss of historic features.

ATCHISON COUNTY, Atchison
1896-1897
George P. Washburn, architect
Latimer & Benning, contractor
Romanesque Revival. Occupies portion of full block two and one-half blocks north of the central business district; limestone walls and trim; prominent iron staircase at east; courtroom has been reoriented from original north-south axis to east-west axis.

BARTON COUNTY, Great Bend
1917-1918
W. E. Hulse & Co., architect
Manhattan Construction Co., contractor
"Modern (classical) Eclecticism." Occupies double block square surrounded by the central business district; stone faced walls and trim, original monumental entrance staircase was replaced in 1952 by on-grade entrance with modern detailing; courtroom remodeled.

BOURBON COUNTY, Fort Scott
1929-1930
Cuthbert & Suehrk, architect
Thogmartin and Reis, contractor
"Modern (classical) Eclecticism." Occupies full block square one block west of the central business district; brick with limestone trim; barrel-vaulted courtroom contains mural painting of "Justice Enthroned" by D. H. Overmeyer (1929); law enforcement facility has been added to north.

Barton

Bourbon

Brown

Butler

BROWN COUNTY, Hiawatha
1925-1926
W. E. Hulse, architect
Harvey Wood, contractor
"Modern (classical) Eclecticism." Occupies full block square surrounded by the central business district; limestone walls and trim; notable decorative carvings on exterior; interior public spaces are highly ornamented; courtroom has coved ceiling lighted indirectly; unobtrusive installation of elevator at southwest corner of building in 1980-1981.

BUTLER COUNTY, El Dorado
1908-1909
George P. Washburn & Sons, architect
Matheim & Walker, contractor
Romanesque Revival. Occupies full block square adjacent to the west arm of the central business district; red brick with limestone trim; "Justice" crowns main entrance portico; courtroom floor has been redesigned; new judicial building constructed immediately to east in 1971.

Chase

Chautauqua

CHASE COUNTY, Cottonwood Falls
1871-1873
John Haskell, architect
James Bannon, contractor
Second Empire/"Franco-American." Occupies full block square which terminates the south end of the main commercial street; limestone walls and trim; pressed metal ceilings; winder staircase; tower rebuilt in 1966.

CHAUTAUQUA COUNTY, Sedan
1917-1918
Washburn & Sons, architects
N. B. Niblong, contractor
"Modern (classical) Eclecticism." Occupies full block square two blocks north of the central business district; red brick with stone trim; courtroom has sloped floor; courtroom ceiling has been lowered.

Cheyenne

Clay

CHEYENNE COUNTY, St. Francis
1924-1925
Thomas Williamson & Co., architect
Thomas Howard, contractor
"Modern (classical) Eclecticism." Occupies full block square at east end of the central business district; light buff brick with limestone trim; tinted windows and blank transom panels have replaced original window units.

CLAY COUNTY, Clay Center
1900-1901 (preliminary plans 1898)
J. C. Holland, architect
Ziegler & Dalton, contractors
Romanesque Revival. Occupies full block square surrounded by the central business district; limestone walls and trim; lincrusta walton wainscoting; courtroom altered; jail of contemporary date (with 1980-1981 addition) at southeast corner of square.

Comanche

Crawford

COMANCHE COUNTY, Coldwater
1927-1928
Routledge & Hertz, architect
Thomas Howard, contractor
"Modern (classical) Eclecticism." Occupies full block square one block south of main east-west axis of the central business district; courtroom and other public spaces remain substantially unaltered.

CRAWFORD COUNTY, Girard
1921-1922
Tonini & Bramblet, architect
J. J. Rooney, contractor
"Modern (classical) Eclecticism." Occupies full block square surrounded by the central business district; limestone walls and trim; courtroom has coved ceiling and paired corinthian columns; elevator has been inserted into central atrium (stained glass skylight).

Decatur

DECATUR COUNTY, Oberlin
1926-1927
Squires and Ross, architect
Cork & Ferrier, contractor
"Modern (classical) Eclecticism." Occupies southern portion of a block which forms the east side of the central business district; orange brick with stone trim; windows replaced and elevator inserted in west end (1980-1981).

Doniphan

DONIPHAN COUNTY, Troy
1905-1906
G. P. Washburn & Son, architect
J. H. Waggenbrecht, contractor
Romanesque Revival hybrid. Occupies full block square surrounded by Troy's central business district; red brick with limestone trim; the site has been adorned with more memorials than most courthouse squares, including a monumental wood sculpture of a native American carved in 1978 by Peter Toth.

Douglas

DOUGLAS COUNTY, Lawrence
1903-1904
Haskell & Gunn, architect
Cuthbert & Sargent, contractor
Romanesque Revival. Occupies portion of block at south end of Lawrence's central business district; limestone walls and trim; the exterior masonry work exhibits considerable diversity; the courtroom contains a balcony; a stained-glass dome graces the lobby; extensive interior renovations executed in 1978-1980; law enforcement center erected to east in 1974.

Edwards

EDWARDS COUNTY, Kinsley
1928-1929
Routledge & Hertz, architect
Roy Hatfield, contractor
"Modern (classical) Eclecticism." Occupies a full block square surrounded by residential properties several blocks northwest of the central business district; blond brick with stone trim; the courtroom has stone-faced walls and is decorated with wall pilasters and an ornamental frieze; an elevator has been inserted in main stairwell.

Elk

ELK COUNTY, Howard
1907-1908
George McDonald, architect
Morse Contracting Company, contractor
Romanesque Revival hybrid. Occupies a full block square one block east of the central business district; yellow brick with limestone trim; original main entrance now filled with an elevator; courtroom floor entirely redesigned; some tiled fireplace mantels remain.

Ellis

ELLIS COUNTY, Hays
1940-1942 (WPA)
Mann & Company, architect
"Modern (classical) Eclecticism" hybrid. Occupies a full block square adjacent to the central business district; post rock with granite trim; courtroom adorned with decorative eagles; courthouse square considerably built up with library, new law enforcement center, parking lots.

Finney

FINNEY COUNTY, Garden City
1928-1929
Routledge & Hertz, architect
Bailey-Burns, contractor
"Modern (classical) Eclecticism." Occupies full block square a block west of the central business district; limestone walls and trim; art deco detailing on exterior; courtroom entirely finished in stone and has lowered ceilings.

Ford

FORD COUNTY, Dodge City
1912-1913
Reul A. Curtis, architect
George A. Shaul, contractor
"Modern (classical) Eclecticism." Occupies one half of block north of the central business district; stone walls and trim; the interior has been extensively remodeled.

Franklin

FRANKLIN COUNTY, Ottawa
1891-1893
George P. Washburn, architect
L. W. Divelbiss, contractor
Romanesque Revival. Occupies a full block square at south end of the central business district; red brick with limestone trim; "Justice" surmounts entrance; courtroom has decorative paneled ceiling; new judicial center has been erected to the northeast.

Geary

GEARY COUNTY, Junction City
1899-1900
J. C. Holland, architect
Ziegler & Dalton, contractor
Romanesque Revival. Occupies ¾ block square just east of the central business district; limestone walls and trim; hip roof of tower has been removed; interior has been extensively remodeled.

Grant

GRANT COUNTY, Ulysses
1929-1930
Smith & English, architect
J. M. Fuller, contractor
"Modern (classical) Eclecticism." Occupies full block square one block east of the central business district; brick with tile trim; exterior is ornamented by tile panels of art deco design; courtroom arranged in hemicycle with the witness chair appearing (like a throne) in the center of the north wall.

Gray

GRAY COUNTY, Cimarron
1927
Routledge & Hertz, architect
Dalton & Hatch, contractor
"Modern (classical) Eclecticism." Occupies full block square south of the central business district; brown brick with limestone trim; courtroom embellished by pilasters.

Greeley

GREELEY COUNTY, Tribune
1889-1890 (old courthouse)
W. T. Heaps, architect
Allen & Oleson, contractor
American Queen Anne hybrid. Occupies full block square one block east of the central business district; stone walls and trim; painted clock face in central gable; new courthouse occupies western portion of the square.

Hamilton

HAMILTON COUNTY, Syracuse
1937
Overend and Boucher, architect
Frank E. Blaser, contractor
"Modern (classical) Eclecticism." Occupies north end of block at the north end of the central business district; blond brick with stone trim; courtroom ceiling has been lowered.

Harper

HARPER COUNTY, Anthony
1907-1908
George P. Washburn, architect
Matheim & Walters, contractor
Romanesque Revival. Occupies full block square one block north of the central business district; red brick with limestone trim; for its age, courthouse is remarkably unaltered, both exterior and interior; courtroom's paneled ceiling ornamented by decorative plasterwork.

Hodgeman

HODGEMAN COUNTY, Jetmore
1929-1930
Routledge & Hertz, architect
William B. Steller, contractor
"Modern (classical) Eclecticism." Occupies full block square surrounded on three sides by the central business district; yellow brick with limestone trim; courtroom embellished by fluted pilasters.

Jackson

JACKSON COUNTY, Holton
1919-1921
Thomas Williamson, architect
Cuthbert & Son, contractor
"Modern (classical) Eclecticism." Occupies full block square surrounded by the central business district; tan brick with stone trim; 1937 wall paintings by V. Barnes, originally located in courtroom, now ornament an office area created when courtroom was shortened.

Jewell

JEWELL COUNTY, Mankato
1936-1937 (WPA, KERC)
Radstinsky & Mertz, architect
"Modernistic." Occupies full block at north end of the central business district; post-rock walls and trim; carved panels adorn front and rear entrances; courtroom ornamented by decorative frieze.

Kearny

KEARNY COUNTY, Lakin
1939 (PWA)
Overend and Boucher, architect
A. W. Soderberg, contractor
"Modern (classical) Eclecticism." Occupies full block square at the north end of the central business district; tan brick with limestone trim; jail added to south in 1964.

Kingman

KINGMAN COUNTY, Kingman
1907-1908
George P. Washburn & Son, architect
Matheim & Walters, contractor
Romanesque Revival hybrid. Occupies west half of residential block one block east of the central business district; red brick with limestone trim; courtroom floor has been redesigned and most offices have been remodeled; original windows have been replaced with metal units and opaque transom panels.

Kiowa

KIOWA COUNTY, Greensburg
1913-1914
J. W. Hulse, architect
Stanley and Calahan, contractor
"Modern (classical) Eclecticism." Occupies full block square one block east of the central business district; tan brick with stone trim; fishscale transom over main entrance; original windows replaced with glass blocks; courtroom remodeled; ceilings lowered.

Lane

LANE COUNTY, Dighton
1930-1931
Mann & Company, architect
H. W. Underhill, contractor
"Modern Eclecticism." Occupies ¼ of block just south of the central business district; yellow brick with limestone trim; courtroom richly ornamented.

Leavenworth

LEAVENWORTH COUNTY, Leavenworth
1911-1913
William Feth, architect
J. B. Betts, contractor
"Modern (classical) Eclecticism." Occupies full block square on a hill several blocks south of the central business district; limestone with glazed terracotta trim; central rotunda with stained-glass dome and scagliola columns; second story has been substantially redesigned; original windows have been replaced by metal units.

Lincoln

LINCOLN COUNTY, Lincoln
1899-1900
C. W. Squires, architect
W. P. Baker, contractor
Romanesque Revival. Occupies full block square adjacent to the east end of the central business district; post rock walls and trim; interior has lowered ceilings; courtroom has been shortened.

Linn

Logan

LINN COUNTY, Mound City
1885-1886
George Ropes, architect
Z. Mentzer, supervisor of construction
American Queen Anne. Occupies full block square at east end of the central business district; pressed metal ceilings throughout; red brick with limestone trim; courtroom has been shortened; modern judicial center, health center, and jail buildings have been built on the square.

LOGAN COUNTY, Russell Springs
1887 (old courthouse)
Alfred Meyer, architect
George D. Kerns, contractor
High Victorian. Occupies irregular block at west edge of Russell Springs; red brick with limestone trim; pressed metal ceilings throughout; 1930 stone addition at rear.

McPherson

Marion

McPHERSON COUNTY, McPherson
1894-1895
J. H. Haskell and J. F. Stanton, architects
James Jack, contractor
Romanesque Revival. Occupies ½ of double square one block west of the central business district; limestone walls and trim; extensively remodeled exterior and interior; courtroom has domical skylight.

MARION COUNTY, Marion
1905-1907
J. C. Holland & Squires, architect
J. B. Betts, contractor
Romanesque Revival. Occupies full block square one block south of the central business district; limestone walls and trim; stone carvings at entrance; lowered ceilings; courtroom partially paneled.

Marshall

Meade

MARSHALL COUNTY, Marysville
1891-1892 (old courthouse)
H. C. Koch, architect
Groves and Hackett, contractor
Romanesque Revival. Occupies full block square several blocks east of the central business district; red brick with terracotta and stone trim; decorative terracotta panels on exterior; new courthouse and judicial center occupy west and south portions of square.

MEADE COUNTY, Meade
1928
Fred Hopper, architect
Louis Riggs, contractor
"Modern (classical) Eclecticism." Occupies ½ of a block square two blocks north of the central business district; red and yellow brick with concrete trim; courtroom ornamented with wall pilasters.

Miami

Mitchell

MIAMI COUNTY, Paola
1897-1899
George P. Washburn, architect
L. W. Divelbiss, contractor (dismissed in 1899)
Romanesque Revival. Occupies full block square ½ block south of the central business district; red brick with limestone trim; polychrome slate roofs sheathe the towers; notable Spanish-American War memorial on interior; new jail to north; considerable preservation-minded renovation work completed in 1977.

MITCHELL COUNTY, Beloit
1901-1902
J. C. Holland, architect
Cuthbert & Sargent, contractors
Romanesque Revival. Occupies full block square at east end of the central business district; post-rock walls with sandstone trim; lincrusta walton wainscoting and pressed metal ceilings in corridors; courtroom and offices remodeled.

Montgomery

MONTGOMERY COUNTY, Independence
1931 (remodeling and expansion of 1886 building)
Cuthbert & Suehrk, architect
F. D. Brewster, contractor
"Modern (classical) Eclecticism." Occupies ½ of block square three blocks east of the main intersection of the central business district; main courtroom is ornamented with composite wall pilasters.

Ness

NESS COUNTY, Ness City
1917-1918
J. C. Holland & Sons, architect
Cuthbert & Sons, contractor
"Modern (classical) Eclecticism." Occupies full block square one block west of the central business district; limestone walls and trim; decorative roundels crown the center at the parapet of each facade; courtroom contains balcony; window transoms have opaque panels.

Norton

NORTON COUNTY, Norton
1929
Cuthbert & Suehrk, architect
Gurtler & Company, contractor
"Modern (classical) Eclecticism." Occupies full block square at east edge of the central business district; brown brick with stone trim; courtroom has shallow barrel-vaulted ceiling, wall pilasters and mural painting of "Justice Enthroned" by D. H. Overmyer (1929) above bench; windows are replacements with opaque transom panels.

Osage

OSAGE COUNTY, Lyndon
1922-1923
W. E. Hulse & Company, architect
Montgomery S. Green, contractor
"Modern (classical) Eclecticism." Occupies full block square at north edge of central business district; 1953 remodeling.

Osborne

OSBORNE COUNTY, Osborne
1907-1908
J. C. Holland & Squires, architect
C. Cork, contractor
Romanesque Revival. Occupies full block square two blocks west of central business district; post rock walls and trim; notable stone carvings at main entrance.

Pawnee

PAWNEE COUNTY, Larned
1918-1919
W. E. Hulse, architect
William Foley, contractor
"Modern (classical) Eclecticism." Occupies full block square at north end of the central business district; blond brick with stone trim; notable monumental staircase and ionic portico; new courtroom has been inserted within the old one, with the left-over space used as an additional courtroom.

Phillips

PHILLIPS COUNTY, Phillipsburg
1912-1913
R. A. Curtis (Curtis Engineering Company), architect
Cuthbert & Sons, contractor
"Modern (classical) Eclecticism." Occupies full block square surrounded by the central business district; limestone walls and trim; stained glass skylight ornaments second story lobby; ceilings have been dropped.

Pottawatomie

POTTAWATOMIE COUNTY, Westmoreland
1884
Hulse and Moses, contractors
Round-arched/"Bracketed." Occupies full block square at west end of the central business district; limestone walls and trim; additions have been made to the original square block; interior ceilings dropped, walls paneled.

Pratt

PRATT COUNTY, Pratt
1923
Mann & Company, architect
Randall & Smith, contractor
"Modern (classical) Eclecticism." Occupies full block square one block east of the central business district; red brick with limestone trim; after 1923 fire destroyed part of courthouse (which had originally been built according to the designs of G. P. Washburn in 1909-10) building was redesigned.

Rawlins

RAWLINS COUNTY, Atwood
1906-1907
Eisentraut, Colby, Pottinger Company, architect
Winters and Short, contractor
Romanesque Revival. Occupies full block square at east end of the central business district; red brick with stone trim; windows have been replaced, ceilings lowered, paneling installed.

Reno

RENO COUNTY, Hutchinson
1929-1931
W. E. Hulse, architect
Blaser, Vollmer and Company, contractor
"Modernistic." Occupies most of a block two blocks west of the central business district; blond brick and limestone; central two-story atrium work area; east courtroom and courtroom lobby adorned with mural paintings; west courtroom has been remodeled and new law enforcement building connects to court house at west.

Republic

REPUBLIC COUNTY, Belleville
1939-1940
Mann & Company, architect
Peterson Construction, contractors
"Modernistic." Occupies full block square surrounded by the central business district; concrete with applied rendering, stone and metal trim; decorative window spandrels; courtroom has lowered ceiling.

Rice

RICE COUNTY, Lyons
1910-1911
J. C. Holland and Son, architect
Cuthbert & Son, contractor
Romanesque Revival. Occupies full block square surrounded by the central business district; red brick and limestone trim; building and grounds substantially remodeled.

Riley

RILEY COUNTY, Manhattan
1905-1906
Holland and Squires, architect
J. B. Betts, contractor
Romanesque Revival. Occupies portion of a block at west end of the central business district; limestone walls and trim; stone carvings at entrance; considerably remodeled on interior; courtroom has been shortened.

Rooks

ROOKS COUNTY, Stockton
1921-1924 (design prepared in 1917)
Frank C. Squires, architect
Cuthbert & Sons, contractor
"Modern (classical) Eclecticism." Occupies portion of block just north of the central business district; limestone walls and trim; murals in commissioners' room; elevator addition to south.

Rush

RUSH COUNTY, La Crosse
1888-1889
L. L. Levering, architect
William T. Heaps, contractor
Romanesque Revival. Occupies full block square one block west of the central business district; red brick with limestone trim; courtroom ceiling is coved and sheathed with pressed metal; roof of square tower has been removed; interior remodeled.

Saline

SALINE COUNTY, Salina
1910-1911 (old courthouse)
Wilmarth & Zerbe, architect
J. B. Betts, contractor
"Modern (classical) Eclecticism." Occupies square several blocks west of the central business district; limestone walls and trim; courtroom is ornamented by wall pilasters and elaborate cornice and has been shortened.

Scott

SCOTT COUNTY, Scott City
1924
Mann & Company, architect
Henderson & Riggs, contractor
"Modern (classical) Eclecticism." Occupies full block square one block north and west of the central business district; red brick with limestone trim; courtroom virtually unaltered with decorative wall panels and pilasters.

Sedgwick

SEDGWICK COUNTY, Wichita
1888 (old courthouse)
W. R. McPherson, architect
W. H. Sternberg, contractor
Romanesque Revival. Occupies full block square north of the central business district; statues of "Justice" surmount east and west entrances; considerable recent remodeling; tower has been shortened; exterior steps restored; elaborate GAR memorial at south.

Sheridan

SHERIDAN COUNTY, Hoxie
1917-1918
Thomas W. Williamson, architect
George Cope and Sons, contractor
"Modern (classical) Eclecticism." Occupies full block square one block northwest of the central business district; buff brick with limestone trim; stained-glass panel at stair landing of second story depicts "Justice Enthroned."

Sherman

SHERMAN COUNTY, Goodland
1931
Routledge & Hertz, architect
Blaser & Vollmer, contractor
"Modern (classical) Eclecticism." Occupies ⅓ of double block square one block east of the central business district; blond brick with stone trim; art deco tilework ornaments exterior; courtroom's frieze and cornice use art deco motifs; interior has been somewhat reconfigured.

Smith

SMITH COUNTY, Smith Center
1918-1920
Thomas W. Williamson, architect
M. C. Brady, contractor
"Modern (classical) Eclecticism." Occupies full block square two blocks east of the central business district; limestone walls and trim; recent window replacement.

Stafford

STAFFORD COUNTY, St. John
1928-1929
Mann & Company, architect
"Modern (classical) Eclecticism." Occupies portion of block in the central business district; buff brick and limestone trim; unusual triangular plan; law library has been inserted into old jail.

Stanton

STANTON COUNTY, Johnson City
1925-1926
Smith & English, architect
S. S. Strong, contractor
"Modern (classical) Eclecticism." Occupies full block square at north end of the central business district; multicolored brick with concrete trim; dropped ceilings; courtroom has been paneled.

Thomas

Wallace

Wichita

Wyandotte

THOMAS COUNTY, Colby
1906-1907
J. C. Holland & Squires, architect
L. Crosby & Son, contractor
Romanesque Revival. Occupies site two blocks east of the central business district; red brick with limestone trim; pressed metal ceiling on second floor; courtroom is shortened, has lowered ceilings, paneled walls; windows have been replaced with units that have opaque panels.

WABAUNSEE COUNTY, Alma
1931-1932
W. E. Glover, architect
Shuss & Henderson, contractors
"Modern (classical) Eclecticism." Occupies full block square on hill two blocks west of the central business district; limestone walls and trim; decorative window spandrels; courtroom is barrel vaulted with decorative acoustical ceiling tiles and paintings on the rear wall.

WALLACE COUNTY, Sharon Springs
1914-1915
W. E. Hulse & Company, architect
William Foley, contractor
"Modern (classical) Eclecticism." Occupies full block square at north end of the central business district; buff brick with concrete trim; pressed metal ceilings.

WASHINGTON COUNTY, Washington
1932-1934
H. G. Overend & C. F. Boucher, architect
Blaser & Vollmer, contractors
"Modern (classical) Eclecticism." Occupies full block square surrounded by the central business district; limestone walls and trim; decorative window spandrels; courtroom virtually unaltered with decorative frieze and wall pilasters.

WICHITA COUNTY, Leoti
1916-1917
W. E. Hulse & Company, architect
William Foley, contractor
"Modern (classical) Eclecticism." Occupies full block square one block south of the central business district; red brick with concrete trim; lowered ceilings.

WOODSON COUNTY, Yates Center
1899-1900
George P. Washburn, architect
J. W. Brewsler, contractor
Romanesque Revival. Occupies full block square surrounded by the central business district; red brick and limestone trim; courtroom has decorative paneled ceiling; cupola has been altered; stone trim painted white; enclosures built to protect basement entrances.

WYANDOTTE COUNTY, Kansas City
1925-1927
Wight & Wight, architect
Godfrey Swenson, contractor
"Modern (classical) Eclecticism." Occupies ½ of rectangular block west of central business district; limestone walls and trim; two-story, barrel-vaulted hall on third floor; stained-glass windows at landing of main stair; windows have been replaced.

Wabaunsee

Washington

Woodson

Bibliographical Note

For those interested in county courthouses generally, *Court House,* a publication edited by Richard Pare and published by Horizon Press in 1978, provides excellent photographic coverage of the subject using a national perspective. The book also contains several informative essays. Courthouse architecture in the Midwest and Texas is the subject of a 1970 dissertation by Paul Goeldner entitled "Temples of Justice," which is available from University Microfilms International, Ann Arbor, Mich.

Information on county courthouses in Kansas can be obtained from a variety of sources. However, caution must be observed as a number of published materials have not proven to be entirely reliable. The library catalog at the Kansas State Historical Society records many of the sources available on the subject. Newspaper accounts dating to the period when a courthouse was being proposed, constructed, and/or dedicated can be entertaining and valuable sources of information. The Society's collections also include the WPA-sponsored Historical Records Survey, which contains much useful material pertaining to a number of county courthouses. Visiting courthouses may also repay the time and expense involved—the original plans and specifications for the building as well as commissioners' journals are still available for inspection in some cases.

For more information on the architectural history of county courthouses one must consult a variety of sources for the most balanced coverage. Critical writings and popular handbooks on architecture which date from the period when a given building was constructed are very good sources of information about the aesthetic and philosophical ideals prevalent at the time. Marcus Whiffen's guide to architectural styles, *American Architecture Since 1780,* and his more recent *American Architecture 1607-1976* (with Frederick Koeper as coauthor), give an overview of trends in American architecture as well as useful bibliographies. J. Kurt von Achen's unpublished Master's thesis, "Lives and Works of Early Kansas Architects" (University of Kansas, School of Architecture, 1966), may also be of interest.

Acknowledgements

This project was initiated by the Historic Preservation Department of the Kansas State Historical Society in 1979. Despite many setbacks it has come to fruition through the hard work, persistence, and helpful assistance of many persons.

Jeff Wampler spent the summer of 1979 searching out information on county courthouses in all of Kansas' 105 counties. Through his work the basic database for the project was formed. The staff of the various departments of the Kansas State Historical Society were continually helpful and patient. Their familiarity with the Society's collections resulted in a number of suggestions which did much to strengthen the project. Members of several local historical societies responded promptly to queries with contributions of factual material. Finally, county officers and employees proved to be willing sources of badly needed information, tolerant of inconvenient requests for assistance, and good-humored subjects for the camera.

Garfield county, annexed to Finney county in 1893